MARILYN

amanda ngoho reavey

THE OPERATING SYSTEM PRINT//DOCUMENT

Marilyn

ISBN-10: 0986050539
ISBN-13: 978-0-9860505-3-4

Cover from paintings by Joo Young Choi, used with permission from the artist
Front: "grow, grow, grow"
Back: "blue girl is on fire or disappearing from judgmental flesh houses"
Please find more work and information at http://jooyoungchoi.com

"The Same Old Figurative," a poem by Joel M. Toledo, from his book The Long Lost Startle
appears by permission by the poet and his publisher, University of the Philippines Press.

This text was set in HWT Geometric, Franchise, Minion, Marion and OCR A Standard,
printed and bound by Spencer Printing and Graphics
in Honesdale, PA, in the USA.

Operating System Publications are distributed to the trade
by Small Press Distribution / SPD.

Library of Congress Control Number 2015915580

First Edition

THE OPERATING SYSTEM//PRESS
141 Spencer Street #203
Brooklyn, NY 11205
www.theoperatingsystem.org

MARILYN

amanda ngoho reavey

AN OPERATING SYSTEM PUBLICATION
Brooklyn, New York

DEDICATION

For

Meaghan Owens

"What time is it, I mean to say where am I, I mean to say where have I gone - I don't know anymore, in this instant when I call out to myself, where I'm passing or where I'm going."

~ Hélène Cixous, "What is it O'Clock? Or the Door (We Never Enter)," *Stigmata: Escaping Texts.*

"ikaw gapugos pagbuklad
a maitom ug gunsongong
yuta nga ang kasing-kasing
kahilitan."

"you are breaking open s
the dark and coarse
earth whose heart
is a desert."

~Hi-D Palapar, "Alang sa Ninglangyaw, Gikan sa Naghuwat"

"'Reverse migration. . .' Is psychotic."

~Bhanu Kapil, Schizophrene
[In July 2013, I ask her to sign my copy. She quotes the above from her book, then writes next to it: DISCUSS.]

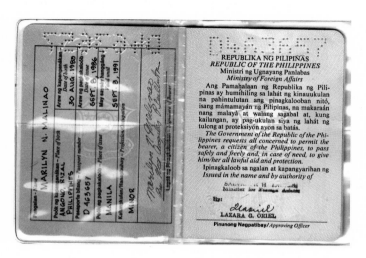

Pangalan / *Name*
MARILYN N. MALINAO

Poók ng kapanganakan – *Place of Birth*
ANGONO, RIZAL PHILIPPINES

Araw ng kapanganakan – *Date of Birth*
30 AUG 1988

Pasaporte bilang – *Passport number*
D 465657

Araw ng pagkakaloób – *Date of issue*
SEPT 8, 1986

Poók ng pagkakaloób – *Place of issue*
MANILA

May saysay hanggang – *Valid until*
SEPT 8, 1991

Kah. Kudan/Hanapbuhay – *Profession/Occupation*
MINOR

Lagda ng May-ari/ Signature of Bearer

REPUBLIKA NG PILIPINAS
REPUBLIC OF THE PHILIPPINES
Ministri ng Ugnayang Panlabas
Ministry of Foreign Affairs

Ang Pamahalaan ng Republika ng Pilipinas ay humihiling sa lahát ng kinauukulan na pahintulutan ang pinagkalooban nitó, isang mámamayán ng Pilipinas, na makaraán nang malayà at walang sagabal at, kung kailangan, ay pag-ukulan siya ng lahát ng tulong at proteksiyón ayon sa batás.

The Government of the Republic of the Philippines requests all concerned to permit the bearer, a citizen of the Philippines, to pass safely and freely and, in case of need, to give him/her all lawful aid and protection.

Ipinagkaloob sa ngalan at kapangyarihan ng
Issued in the name and by authority of

SALVADOR H. LAUREL
Minister for Foreign Affairs

By:
LAZARA G. ORIEL

Pinunong Nagpatibay/ *Approving Officer*

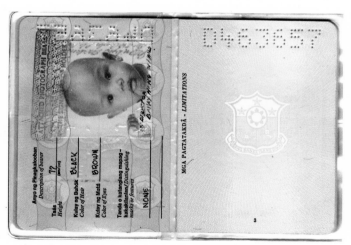

Anyo ng Pinagkalooban
Description of bearer

Taás – *Height*
172

Kulay ng Buhók – *Color of Hair*
BLACK

Kulay ng Matá – *Color of Eyes*
BROWN

Tandâ o katanging mapag-kakakilanlan/ *Distinguishing marks or features*
NONE

MGA PAGTATAKDÂ - *LIMITATIONS*

3

MARILYN

MARILYN

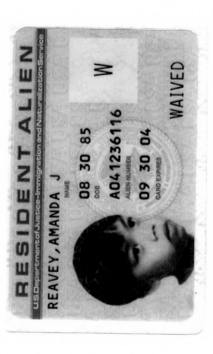

PRELUDE: EMIGRANT NOTES on POSSESSION
written after lighting my "Resident Alien" card on fire

1. Two days after turning 8 years old, the papers were signed and she left her name.
When she left her name, she left her country.

2. For an emigrant a desire line is a kind of violence that masks loneliness.
How the body appears whole but is secretly – suspended – mid flight – a hand that stops a
plucked string from making sound.

3. Sometimes the only choice is to flee or to merge.
To flee is to dissociate. To merge is a kind of possession.

4. For example, as an adult, she traveled the Silk Road from Rome to Istanbul.
Gave away her fingers and toes to lovers until she had none.

5. Once she found her mother's handwritten signature and right thumbmark forgotten in
the back of a closet. Immediately she bought a black inkpad.
Made marks all over the paper. How there might be similarities in the looped lines.
How shadows make the light tangible.

6. Identity is a Freudian slip. She says, "hold me." He says, "what are you hungry for."

7. She puts her thumb on top of her mother's thumbmark. On an inhale. Her body slips
through time and into hers. All at once she understands
how orphan children are never born. How they – simply – appear.

8. She stares at him. The way she stares at people when she can't understand what they're
saying and tries to fill in the gaps instead of asking them to repeat themselves.

9. Could we converse instead in color and brushstrokes? For example, mix burnt Siena
and white. Take a palette knife. Make dark marks that dent the blank canvas.

10. Yesterday, she made a tea her mother used to make. Put it in a pint-sized mason jar.
Put it on her tongue. To drink. Instead. She drank a memory.

11. It tasted of Sulawesi sea salt and a bloody handprint. Smeared across white washed
walls. A crimson line on cobblestone dragged out the back gate of the courtyard.
Afterwards, she threw the mason jar in the alleyway.
It stopped – mid flight – it did not shatter. It did not sound.

I . TESSERAE

tes.ser.a: (*pl. tesserae*) a small tile or glass used in making a mosaic.

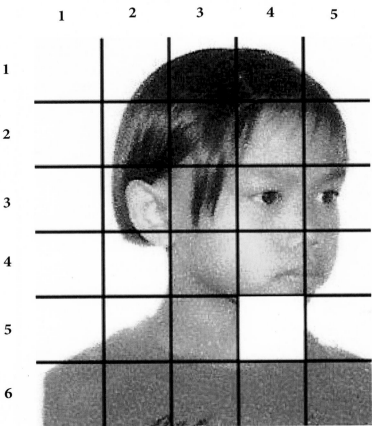

Fig 1.1

voice: a sound produced in the larynx and uttered through the mouth of the living to express something in words.

My wanting is not the grid's wanting.

TUESDAY

It started with walking. But I wonder if most things start with walking.

Walking. Towards red.   The catalyst.

Fear.

Not finding red. Instead. Abyss. Abysmal. A bay. A bahay. A bahay kubo. In Cebuano, this means "house-cube." It is a house-on-stilts. My friend's uncle won't leave the bamboo house-on-stilts.

Where am I going? I am getting there.

In the jungle there is a foreboding that surrounds a sentence. It lactates. It drowns.

They say that by the time a child is one year old her brain has been wired to know

and understand only the phonemes of the language that surrounds her.

I spent eight years in speech therapy learning how English letters and words should be formed in my mouth. Hollow. The tip of the tongue placed behind the back of the top teeth. Bared. Legs - I mean, lips - spread. A slight vibration as the air pushes out. Unlike Tagalog, the 'S' is voiceless. Like the /s/ in 'self.' Or 'citizen.'

But what if you have something to say and can't understand an English tongue?

A barefoot girl in a black dress twirls in the moonshine.

Will English never be mine?

Last night I cried myself to sleep. Dreamt I was barefoot on red soil. Climbing a balete tree. Someone called my name: Marilyn. A tin roof and no windows. To keep the cool inside. Humidity out. Humility. Tropical architecture is tricky.

In 2011, I returned to the Philippines. Took a 14-hour ferry from Cebu to Iloilo, then a 15-minute pumpboat to Guimaras. Where they are famous for their mangos. They trade them. Below a 20-foot cross that lights up at night.

This man. I picked him up in a basement bar. Fervent with theatre lights. He wants to know more about this relationship. To place. To place something. To find place. To find self in place. To self. To identity. To water. To family. To mangos.

Yes, I desire to know more too.

I hate mangos.

Meeeennngggooooohhhh. That is how my friend says it. She is a writer from Cebu. Met her for the first time while living in Italy, having won a scholarship to study fine arts on the outskirts of Pistoia. And later, in Greece. On a beautiful island called Paros. Five hours by ferry from Athens. Reminds me of Manila. Gritty.

In Athens, we dance with transients in Monasteraki. We bum cigarettes. And Mythos, a kind of beer. Children hold out an empty palm and a yellow rose. They ask: *Tha thélate na agorásete éna louloúdi?* Would you like to buy a flower? It is late, but they are not allowed to go home until the roses are sold. We cannot afford to pay them.

Malakas. The first Greek word I learned. It means 'bastard.'
But in Tagalog it means 'one who is strong.'

The children fall asleep in our laps.

In 2011, my friend invited me to the Philippines to stay with her and her family. I was afraid, but went anyway. Alone. From Chicago to Toronto. Toronto to Hong Kong. Hong Kong to Manila. Manila to Cebu. My first time back since leaving.

It was important. To leave alone and to return alone. The first time I left, I left alone.

During that trip I also visited Melbourne. From the plane I marveled over the blue mountains near Sydney. Blue haze ripples.

In Melbourne, I re-met my foster family. My foster mother's living room matches my adopted mother's kitchen. They have never met.

My foster mother called me Marilyn Malinao. I said I am Amanda Reavey now. She apologized; she felt we had bonded because we had had the same first name.

We sat down and had a family dinner with all of my foster siblings. Except one. Because he lives in Singapore. She made chicken adobo.

I did not like traveling alone in Asia. Because they expected my skin to be my culture. And they teased me. Presumably, in Tagalog. Or Cebuano. Or Ilocano. I don't know. I was often detained in airports, in a small room with flickering fluorescent lighting: how did I come to have an American passport? What kind of black magic is this? Whom did you pay? And with what?

As a child, I used to run away instead of opening my mouth because I couldn't articulate anything.

fuckyou

I only ever made it to the end of the driveway. The line like a border.

The one-night stand is still lying in my bed as I sit at my desk to write. He asks me about shifting, my avoidance of mother. I shift towards him, in my seat, and cross my legs. A body shifts when language shifts. Birth mother has no place in English.

Her name was (is)

Anahaw palms and buko pie and balete trees and sitting along the dirt road drinking San Miguel stolen from one of the sari-sari shops that line the paved street.

Memories stagnate.

She was 13.

When the bottles empty, we fill them with water from the community faucet at the end of the road.

She would have been (will be) 41. This year.

I want to tell him: ask Marilyn the rest. I don't (want to) remember anymore.

Last night I dreamt of Paros. The awakening after the first night of living there. Of a neighbor. Who was raped that night. I will never forget hanging my laundry on the courtyard clothesline. The obliviousness. The moment before is always extraordinary. Before noticing the blood. The look and smell of blood on white-washed walls and cobblestone. The little old Greek lady attempting to wash it away with Aegean seawater and a mop.

My friend's uncle smoked cigarettes and twitched. The entire time I was there he refused to leave the bahay kubo. Once, he pinched my skin. I went inside the main house. Took a bucket bath. With rain water. Lizards watched me.

Every place I have lived that starts with a 'P' I have both loved and hated.
Philippines. Pistoia. Paros. Paris.

I saved up all my money from a temp job and moved. To a third floor walk up. The only thing in the apartment in English was my roommate's Bible. She used to quiz me. And we went to Church a lot. Because someone on the second floor was doing black magic. We were both convinced this person sent the pigeons to watch us. Swarms of them hung outside the west windows. Watching.

I lived on coffee and biscuits and cigarettes. We did our laundry in the bathtub and hung it on hangers in the windows, which faced a seminary. Would the monks get distracted during their walking meditations? Would they look up?

My saving grace was a second-hand English bookstore and tea room near the Luxembourg Gardens. Dusty, water-damaged books. The proprietor, a woman who had fled her native Germany to escape the Nazis, held a James Joyce book club every Wednesday night in the tea room, separated from the rest by a yellow, almost transparent curtain.

I used to sit up straight in my bed sweating from night terrors. My roommate blessed the windows.

The plumbing broke. Twice. Water leaked into the neighbor's apartment below us. He banged on the door: *Je vous connais déjà les américains! J'ai vécu cinq ans à New York!* I know what you Americans are like! I lived in New York for five years!

I replied: *Ah, vraiment? Et comment vous les trouvez, ces américains? Je ne suis jamais allée à New York.* Oh, really? And what are these Americans like? I have never been to New York.

Malakas.

My roommate and I had to take bucket baths. Our British landlady, a Londoner, said we could dump the water out the south window into the courtyard. Once she came for tea and asked, "which part of London are you from?" I didn't correct her. Or tell her about speech therapy. Or about my adopted father, who is English, who has relatives all over the UK and Europe.

Instead, the words 'Haringey' and 'Tottenham' rolled off my tongue.

The following summer, I moved to Rome. To an apartment near the Basilica di Santa Maria Maggiore. I became more English, donning an accent I had when I was seven, in order to get a job as a bartender at The Fiddler's Elbow, an Irish bar where I read an English translation of Dostoevsky's The Brothers Karamazov in the back corner, lit shots on fire, and drank them through straws.

I met a new lover from Moscow and began a failed attempt to learn Russian while at the same time studying Italian. At Cin-Cin in the Piazza Venezia. I gave €4 to the cashier and brought my receipt to the counter: *Un espresso doppio, per favore, et anche un cornetto cioccolato.*

The flames parched my throat.

Salamat. I mean, thank you. I mean, *merçi beaucoup.* I mean, *efharistó.* I mean, *grazie.*

WEDNESDAY

Hungry. Woke up realizing I hadn't eaten since 3:30PM on Monday. Of all things, hunger is easiest. After initial pains, it subsides to a dull ache. Eventually, the rumbling stops. The headaches disappear. Everything dissipates. Hiiiiiisssss. The body learns to tolerate absence.

Afraid of the dark, a daisy retreats at night. When the noises emerge. Even the house maid is afraid.

Her son and husband died. She keeps her 14-year-old daughter close. Does not allow her to go to school. She is afraid of losing her.

But you are so smart, I think, *you deserve to go to school. You are a year older than my mother was.*

My first father - I typed 'father' instead of foster - is this important? I was told never erase my Freudian slips.

Nino. Ninoy. Noynoy. In Manila, this is everyone's pet name for Benigno Aquino. The beloved. I speak of him as if I loved him. As if I had been old enough. He was assassinated nine days before I might have been born.

In *Under the Tuscan Sun*, there is a line: "Assassino. No, I did not say 'assassino.' I said, 'Ask Nino.'"

I believe survival is not about hunger. Nor nourishment. Nor hope. Nor anger. Nor love. It is about curiosity.

My friend reminds the housemaids that though I look Filipina, I can't speak the language. She reminds me they might forget.

Her house sits perched atop a canyon. On the outskirts of Cebu. Part of the Visayas. In central Philippines. At night the walls echo. Tokó croak. Jungle crows. Cock fights. Monkeys. It is noisier than New York City or any metropolis at night. There is a rat in my room that likes to chew on the black plastic bags. I nicknamed him 'Ratatouille.'

Despite living in a canyon, water is scarce. Everything is done with rain water: cooking, cleaning, drinking, bathing, washing clothes. I love the smell of the jungle after it rains. The sharpness of greens and yellows momentarily vibrant and tolerable. The dampness hits your face and opens the eyes for dreaming.

Vinegar.
Animal.
Tilling.
Resin.
Shit.
Coffee.
Singing.
Herbaceous.
Vegetal.
Sunlight.
Dirt.
Salt.
Sweat.
Clarity.

If there wasn't enough rain in the rain barrels, they used water from the faucet. This is a new commodity. A pipe was installed a couple years ago. A line running from the community faucet a half mile away, at the end of the dirt road where children play basketball. Occasionally, they take breaks to hold their mouths under the water. The little ones run their hands through the mud. Laughing.

I hear my yaya singing.

Dreams masquerade as memory.

In my last foster home, the maids kept a bowl of cooked rice in the pantry to snack on throughout the day. I used to open the door and drag the bowl out into the light of the kitchen.

"Reavey" is the Anglicized form of the Gaelic "O'Riabhaigh."
It means "brindled," "grizzled."

Twelve years ago my family and I went to Ireland to meet relatives and research family origins. Hanging upside down we kissed the Blarney Stone. We touched the North Sea. Roamed the streets of Belfast. We saw the library at Trinity
College and the Book of Kells, the calligraphy swooping down the page like vines. We touched the soil. My cousin, 11 years old at the time, cried and said, "Do you feel it, Amanda? The land. Our ancestors came from here."

I smiled, "yes, yes. I feel it too."

Later I took a walk alone in an old cemetery down the street in Swords. There was a Celtic cross grave marker with worn etchings surrounded by a rusted iron-wrought fence and overgrowth. I wanted to touch it. This beautiful, forgotten grave marker.

Wanting towards. My wanting is not the grid's wanting. Marilyn, remember your name. Malinao, remember your story.

Name and story and tribe are the same thing. A name is a story and a story is the tribe's identity. *Malinao*. It means 'clear.' From a phrase in Bikol-naga: *malinao na isip*. Because my ancestors had such 'clear thoughts,' they birthed an island.

I cannot give birth to an island.

But today I am thinking about reaching. When we were in Northern Ireland I saw the mythological site where a giant attempted to cross the sea to reach his lover, separated by wars. His bones lay scattered. Like Tristan and Yseult, he felt betrayed and died of grief. She died mourning his soul. There grows hazel and honeysuckle, intertwined and bleeding.

What happens if (when) the reaching is never reached? Do you keep reaching anyway? He knew he would drown. Is hope the emotion that un-grounds us?

I googled this last question. Third link from the top was the definition of Borderline Personality Disorder. According to about.com, "BPD is associated with strong sensitivity to abandonment, which includes intense fear of being abandoned by loved ones and attempts to avoid real or imagined abandonment."

What is the space inside the borderline?

Dreamt I ran out of the house. A woman mixed a red paste in a coconut bowl. She put it upside down on my head and the paste dripped down my face.

I realized it was blood.

In a poem called "Alang sa Ninglangyaw, Gikan sa Naghuwat," Hi-D Palapar asks the emigrant in Cebuano: *nganong dili makit-an sa imong nasudang imong garbo?*

As if to prove her point, she translates it into English:

For the one who left, from the one left behind.

Can you not take pride in your country?

A woman approaches me, screaming. She does not recognize me with my blood-stained skin. I tell her: it's me. Amanda. She is suspicious, but stops screaming. I tell her: you named me 'Marilyn.' She makes a sharp turn and walks away.

THURSDAY

It rained last night. Dreamt I was in a tower. The tower swayed. Seasick, I held onto a chair hinged to the floor. Someone jumped from the main structure. From which the tower had unhinged itself. Into the room. He sat down to tell me a story. I thought, I should wake myself up so I can write what he says.

But sleep had returned from a two day absence and the covers were warm.

A friend places a single white sheet of paper in the rain. As if to soak up the channel that had gathered between sidewalks.

Once, after a night of playing drinking games and losing Rummikub at Meltemi, a bar along the coast of the Aegean Sea, a friend had a panic attack. I asked if he was okay. He said he didn't want to talk to me because I couldn't possibly understand the pressures parents put on their children. Because I didn't actually have a family.

My parents were not my real parents.

I decided he deserved to have that panic attack. I hoped he would have another one.

When I arrived in the Philippines, we took a jeepney from the airport in Cebu and drove along the coast. It was early morning. Humid. Salty. Silver slivers on the water. Someone is sleeping in a hammock tied between the tires of someone else's truck. A fisherman puts on his sadok, then rows out in a small blue bangka. He casts a net.

I ask my friend, "what is this sea called?"

She says,

"what is your obsession with having a name, or a word, for everything?"

Rummikub is a tile game. I am thinking of tesserae, the tiles that make up a mosaic.

I loved the darkness of the sea at night. The only sound was the ferry horn. And the white caps of waves (the goats are jumping) crashing against the rocks. And a fisherman slamming octopi against Parian marble. To tenderize it. I saw my first shooting star.

How can you define it without a name? How can you know where it's placed?

I remember showing my mother a white bear and a brown bear:

"which one do you like better?"

The stars are like tesserae. In the absence of artificial light, one can see stars and orient to them. They coalesce into a constellation. I ask a friend which way is east and she points to Orion's Belt. I sing a Tagalog song for travelers.

In the Philippines, the first thing I notice is everyone looks like me.

I hear my yaya singing.

The moon shines sharply at night. The edges shimmer.

My yaya once wrote a letter. On A4 pink paper. The lines were college ruled. She wrote it to my adoptive family in all capital letters.

She said every morning I would wake up and cry and cry and cry. Until someone came for me. Because that's what Marilyn is.

Usually, the adoptive family has to go to the adoptee's country of origin. But I came to them instead. Because of the revolution. Thousands of families gathered in the Epifanio de los Santos highway. They sang *Bayan Ko*, my country, and wore yellow ribbons. The tanks made the ground tremble. Children held out a palm and a yellow rose: would you like to buy a flower? Nuns placed white sampaguitas in the barrels of aiming guns and prayed the rosary.

These are just things I've heard. I wasn't actually there. But I lived near enough to feel how the earth moved under my feet and up my body.

A barefoot girl in a black dress twirls in the moonshine.

Do not ask me about loneliness. Ask me instead about the blueness of stars.

I arrived at the airport in Denver on December 5. I wore a pink linen dress. Pink plastic shoes. I had a passport, papers and a doll.

Looking out the window, I saw white rice everywhere. In the Philippines, there is no word for 'snow.'

My mother's favorite number is 5. Because she was born on April 5. Her wedding anniversary is on February 5. I came to the US on December 5.

Every year my parents' birthdays and my birthday fall on the same day of the week.

In 2011, when I reunited with my second foster family, I found out my birthday is actually one day later than I thought. The orphanage had decided my birthday based on where I was developmentally. I called my mother.

She looked through the blue folder that held all my immigration and adoption papers. "No, no," she said. "Your birthday is still the 30th."

I don't believe in documentation. Depending on the document, I could have been born in 5 different cities scattered among 3 different islands

The degree of blackness is completely relative. I look at my notes sitting on my desk. Someone has taken a yellow highlighter to it. No, it is the sunlight through the blinds. Or am I hallucinating light?

I need one more country. One more country and I can say I have lived in seven different countries. My favorite number is seven.

Joel M. Toledo wrote one of my favorite poems. I should cut it up. Bury it. See what grows.

What is it about hope. And trust. I am afraid I will get gulped up by the moonshine. Will the moonshine swallow me whole? Or one tessera at a time?

"Yes, the world is strange, riddled with difficult sciences
and random magic. But there are compensations, things we do

perceive: the high cries and erratic spirals of sparrows,
the sky gray and now giving in to the regular rain.

Still we insist on meaning, that common consolation
that, now and then, makes for beauty. Or disaster.

Listen. The new figures are simply those of birds,
the whole notes of their flightless bodies now snagged

on the many scales of the city. And it's just some thunder,
the usual humming of wires. It is only in its breaking

that the rain gives itself away. So come now and assemble
with the weather, notice the water gathering on your cupped

and extended hands — familiar and wet and meaningless.
You are merely being cleansed. Bare instead

the scarred heart; notice how its wild human music
makes such sense. Come, the divining

can wait.
Let us examine the wreckage."

~Joel M. Toledo, "The Same Old Figurative"

There is an image inside my head: a shadow. It pushes into my chest cavity. I think it might rip out my heart. Instead this shadow holds it. Feels it contours.

May I at least throw up the moonshine?

The other day I went to a café with a friend. We watched a drunk man cross the street. He almost got hit by a bus. My friend kept whispering, "wait, wait. Please, please wait."

I thought, this is all we need. After sharing traumas over coffee. To see this man get run over by a bus.

What is a body before it becomes just a body?

In September, where I live now in Colorado, it rains until the creek floods and the levees break. The news sources call it the 100-year flood. My studio apartment is under a foot water. Mud and rocks and garbage and water turn my street into a river and I am forced to evacuate. I couch surf for two weeks.

A deluge. Philippine monsoon rain. Search for higher ground. A body pulled out of the mud. I cannot speak. I cannot articulate anything.

In July I am moving to Pohnpei in Micronesia. My 7th country.

There is a spot to the left of the center of my chest. Near my shoulder. It hurts. I have had it for years. Ever since writing poetry at "the Spot" along Lake Michigan. A red fox sat down next to me. I have a shadow tattoo of a fox on the inside of my left ankle. My fox medicine. My totem. The master of the art of camouflage and adaptability and shapeshifting.

Its medicine means you must become like the wind. I have only experienced two: Meltemi and Scirocco. The scirocco is red. Root chakra. It carries red dust from Africa to Italy.

My friend and I leave the beach hidden by tall grasses. A beach where my cousin and I used to sit to watch the sunrise. As a child, my favorite color was green, like the jungle, and then it was blue. Not a light blue, but a deep one, like the blue of the sea in the distance, just below the horizon. The blue that is almost black.

We make our way back up the hill, straight up, towards the Universe. To discuss what it takes to leave. And to arrive. What does it mean to heal?

I leave my body. She helps me return to it. I have had this pain near my left shoulder since then. A blackness. Another friend said it looked like a weaving. With many layers. I think of a web that makes up the back of a wicker chair. My friend said that during the time I left my body I made a soul agreement to heal the wounds of my blood ancestors. She tells me about yarrow, for violent wounds. We pick some. I put it on my chest.

Last year, I went mustered up the courage to attend the 2nd International Babaylan Conference in Occidental, California. In Visayan, "Babaylan" means "shaman" or "healer."

I learn about dance and drumming. How one might move into a gesture and extend it. Outwards. Until the line moves out of the body.

The redwoods talk to me. I meet a plant whisperer. She teaches me how to pay respect to the *duwende* by leaving an offering. Something given, not stolen.

I pull a small red cloth bundle tied with pink twine from my pocket. Inside is rice from the Banaue rice fields. I scatter it in a circle. I remember my origin story:

Arimaonga, the lion of the sky, attempts to swallow the moon during a lunar eclipse. While my ancestors dance and play drums to scare him away, the Magalos cross the sea with their barongs stained red and kill all but seven women. The Magalos rape, then take the women on their outrigger canoe. Wishing to die rather than become slaves, the women sing canticles. And in these canticles are such 'clear thoughts' (*malinao na isip*) the boat sinks, their captors drown and from the seafloor rises an island.

On the 18-hour plane ride from Toronto to Hong Kong to the Philippines, the sun never rose. Nor set. Rather, it lingered. In an orange-red hue, just above the horizon.

I used to feel the pain in my chest intensely everyday. But now only every so often. When I am moving towards an emotional truth. It subsided to a dull ache on the day my friend and I veered off the highway into a ditch at 80mph. Red.

I left my body again.   Red.

I did not even notice I had left the car.   Red.

That I had started walking barefoot along the side of the highway. Red.

On the gravel.   Red.

Between cement and chicory moon.   Red.

I open my palm. In the center a balete tree grows and the leaves transform into jungle crows.

INTERLUDE: SUTURING TECHNIQUES

she stares at him the way she stares at people when she can't understand what they're saying, and tries to fill in the gaps instead of asking them to repeat rep repeat themselves "Could we converse instead in color and brushstrokes?" for example mix burnt Siena and white her eyes glaze he pulls her to him she em embraces embraces him in her ribcage he extends his tongue outwards she eats his limbs takes a palette knife makes black marks that dent the white canvas he tastes of Sulawesi seasalt it only makes the jungle crow more thirsty knowing there is fresh water in a bamboo stalk she pecks at it until it splits splits open out steps a man named Malakas, meaning 'one who is strong', and a woman named Maganda, meaning 'one who is beautiful' Maganda embrace embraces Malakas in her ribcage he eats her limbs tired, flying for so long on the wind currents there is no place to land she sings a song to make the sea thr throw up rocks that become islands angry, the sky throws down fresh water and a bloody handprint smeared across whitewashed walls a crimson line on cobblestone dragged out the backgate backgate of the courtyard he holds her by the arm, the neck when she resists, he claims to know exactly who she is: "yo "your mother is not here and you are not a not a baby are you a baby?" the second man, a glint in his eye, who is he? he is possessed sometimes the only ch choice is to flee - space out - or to merge if she cannot cannot flee, she must merge to merge is to enact a kind of possession he unzips her pants he unzips his "adults want this," he says identity is a Freudian slip she says, "hold me" he says, "what are you hungry for?" her birth mother's body dragged out

out the backgate of the courtyard they vibrate at their natural frequency in New York, in an attempt to stay, there is a shuffling of documents: adoption paper papers, immigrant papers, an alien number it is hot and the shuffling of tongues tongues unbearable she throws up in a dark gray corner of the American Em Embassy; the U.S. Immigration Officer lables her "distress" upon hearing this story, the the British Embassy gives her a visa because she is seven, she lives with her Aunty and Uncle in Long Wittenham, and sleeps on a cot below a window overlooking the garden once she caught her cousin with a ri a rifle shooting "black bastards" that streamed the sky black carrion crows fell into the violets and green her friends are two white Ebdem geese named Step Stepsy and Stella she is not a citizen: the American Embassy cannot help her she is not a citizen: the Philippine Embassy cannot help her she is not a citizen citizen the British Embassy cannot help her she says, "hold me" he says, "what are you hungry for?" she stares at him, the the way she stares at people who when she can't understand what they're saying "could we converse instead in color and brush strokes?" Make black marks that dent the white paper he unzi unzips her pants ashe eats his limbs identity is a Freudian slip the U.S. Immigration Officer asks, "what is your name?" she replies, "Amanda" he furrows his eyebrows, "it says here your name is Marilyn" she stares at him he continues, "you are not a citizen we cannot help you" some- times she turns the imper imperative into a question when a person, a country, a feeling says, "go"she excitedly pours over maps and imagines what it might be like to live in another another country for example, as an adult, she traveled the Silk Road from Rome to Istanbul gave away her fingers and toes until she had none he says, "wha what are you hungry for?" black carrion crows stream the sky, then fall

into the violets and green wanting towards her wanting is not the grid's wanting yest yesterday, she made made a tea her mother used to make they had to take bucket baths the British landlady, a Londoner, said they could dump the water out out the south window into the courtyard once the sea threw up rocks that became islands and the sky angrily threw down water and flood them once she cam came for tea and asked, "which part of London are you from?" put it in a pint-sized mason jar put it on her tongue to drink instead she drank a memory for

for an emigrant a desire line is a kind of violence that masks loneliness how the body apears whole but is secretly - suspended - mid-flight - a hand that stops stops a plucked string from making sound once she found her mother's handwritten signature and right thumbmark forgotten in the back of a closet immediat mediately she bought a black inkpad made black marks all over the white paper she says, "hold me" he says, "what are you hungry for?" how there might might be similarities in the looped lines how shadows shadows make the light tangible someone calls her name: Marilyn a tin roof and no windws to keep the keep the cool inside humidity out humility tropical architecture is tricky when she was eight years old, she left her name when she left her name, she left her her country she puts her thumb on top of her mother's thumbmark on an inhale her body sleeps through time and into hers all at once she understands how orphan children are never born how they simply appear the space inside the borderline is like the body - the hollow space - of a cello the sky angrily threw up up water she threw up in a dark gray corner of the American Embassy and flooded it it is where the sound resonates it vibrates at its natural frequency how orphan children are never born how they simply appear name and story are the same thing a name is a story the jungle crow pecks and pecks at it until splits splits open out steps a man named Malakas, meaning 'one who is strong' and a woman named Maganda, meaning 'one who is beautiful' a story is the tribe's identity her ancestors sang canticles to make the sea throw up rocks that became islands children hold out an empty palm and a yellow rose would you you like to buy a flower? Do not ask her about loneliness ask her instead about the blueness of stars the plane stopped there is no place to land mid-flight it di it did not sound on the 18-hour plane ride from Toronto to Hong Kong, the sun never rose nor set rather it lingered in an orange-red hue jus just above the horizon the sea threw up rocks that became islands and the sky angrily threw down water and flooded them how there might be similari-ties in

in the looped lines make black marks that dent the white canvas how shadows make the light tangible a friend places a single white sheet of paper in the rain rain as if to soak up the body that had gathered between sidewalks bayan ko her country immediately upon touching the Philippine soil a wave rose within her her "do you feel it Amanda? the land" she smiled, "yes, yes, I feel it too" but it did not recognize her tired of flying for so long on the wind currents there is no place to land islands are like tesserae tesserae coalesce into a mosaic she sings a song to make the sea throw up rocks that become islands her ancestors ancestors sang canticles to make the sea throw up rocks that became islands islands are like tesserae they coalesce into an archipelago she says, "hold me" he says, "what are you hungry for?" her favorite color was green like the jungle then it was blue not a light blue, but a deep one like the blue of the sea in the the distance just below the horizon the blue that is almost black on the plane ride back to the Philippines, the sun never rose nor set rather it lingered in an orange-red hue just above the horizon she sings a song for travelers to make the sea throw up rocks that become islands angry; the sky throws down fresh wat water to flood them, but the bamboo stalks soak it up and the jungle crow, so very thirsty, pecks and pecks the stalks until

it   splits   open

II: AN ARCHITECTURE
of DOORWAYS

AFFIDAVIT OF ACKNOWLEDGMENT

(Both parents or the mother alone may accomplish the Affidavit)

We /I, __ADELIA NGOHO MALINAO__ and _____ parents/
(Father)   (Mother)

parent of the child mentioned in the Certificate of Live Birth, do hereby solemnly swear that the information contained herein
are true and correct to the best of our /my knowledge and belief.

_____	ADELIA NGOHO MALINAO
(Signature of Father)	(Signature of Mother)
Residence Certificate No. _____	Residence Certificate No. 10913551
Date Issued _____	Date Issued July 7, 1986
Place Issued _____	Place Issued Ormoc City

SUBSCRIBED AND SWORN to before me this ____ day of _____, 19 ____

at _____, Philippines.

_____	_____
(Signature of Administering Officer)	(Title / Designation)
_____	_____
(Name in Print)	(Address)

AFFIDAVIT FOR DELAYED REGISTRATION OF BIRTH

(Not applicable for births prior to February 27, 1931 Either the person himself if 21 years old or over, or father / mother / guardian may accomplish the Affidavit)

__Adelia Ngoho Malinao__, of legal age, single / married and with residence and postal
address of __Jaray Boroc, Ormoc City__, after having been duly sworn to in accordance with law,
do hereby depose and say:

1. That I am the applicant for the delayed registration of my birth / of the birth of __Marilyn N. Malinao__
2. That I / he / she was born on __August 10, 1985__
3. That I / he / she is a citizen of __Filipino__
4. That the reason for the delay in registering my / his / her birth was due to __failure to sign form before living__
5. That a copy of my / his / her birth certificate is needed for the purpose of __legal purpose it serve__
6. a. (For the applicant only) That I am married to _____
   b. (For father / mother / guardian) That I am the father / mother / guardian of the said person.

(SGD.) ADELIA NGOHO MALINAO	Residence Certificate No. 10913551-E
(Signature of Affiant)	Date Issued 7/7/86 Place Issued Ormoc City

SUBSCRIBED AND SWORN to before me this __11th__ day of __August__, 19 __86__

at __Quezon City__, Philippines.

_____	(SGD.) ATTY. PIO INCISO
(Signature of Administering Officer)	NOTARY PUBLIC
	PTR 139112
(Name in Print)	

Doc. No. 343

Page No. 67   ISSUED ON 7/13/86

Book No. IV   Quezon City

Series of 1986

HOW TO ACCOMPLISH THIS FORM

1. Accomplish this form in triplicate copies. Upon registration submit the original and duplicate copies to the Local Civil Registrar, and keep the third copy for your personal file.
2. Type or write legibly in ink on the blank spaces provided.
3. Fill up all items in this form completely and accurately.
4. For correctness and accuracy of data, the mother or the father shall be preferred as informant over any other person.

fig 2.1

Anger rises up from the root of me. I want to burn the Deed of Voluntary Surrender. To obscure the signature: the thumbmark. Relegate it to ashes. Bury the ashes in the greenhouse. Next to the lemon tree. Lemons remove toxins from the blood. They purify the body.

I am my mother but I'm not.
I am my grandmother but I'm not.
I am my great-grandmother but I am not.

I use a votive candle from the shrine. My heart contracts and my body clenches. It takes awhile to catch, but then the flames quickly burn through the paper. The imprint of my birth mother's dirt and flesh peels away.

REPUBLIC OF THE PHILIPPINES) S.S.

AFFIDAVIT OF WAIVER

I, _ADELIA N. MALINAO_, Filipino, of legal age _Sin.96_ and
and residing at _Bray Bance, Ormoc City_ after having duly (Civil Status)
sworn to in accordance with law hereby depose and state:

That I am/we are the natural parent (s) of _Marilyn Malinao_,
who was born on _April 30 1985_ at _Ormoc, Ormoc_.

That on _April 28 1986_, I signed a Deed of Voluntary
Surrender wherein I voluntarily and unconditionally surrendered said
child to the care and custody of _HOSPO_ in accordance
with Article 154/155 of Presidential Decree 603 Child Welfare Code;

That I am/we are voluntarily waiving the restoration period
after voluntary commitment and surrender as stated in Article 154 of P.D.
603 since I firmly believe that it will serve his/her best interest in
enhancing her/his normal growth and development;

That his affidavit is executed by me to attest to the veracity
of the foregoing facts and all legal intents and purposes;

FURTHER AFFIANT SAYETH

In witness whereof, I affix my signature this _9th_
day of _July 198 6_ in the _of Ormoc City, Leyte_

Rosita malinao   _Adelia Malinao_
ROSITA M. MALINAO   ADELIA AGONO MALINAO
FATHER GRANDMOTHER   MOTHER
July 9, 1986   _July 8, 1986_

Right Thumbmark   Right Thumbmark

WITNESS:

Elsa N. Bragas   _Judith H. Olsan_

SUBSCRIBED AND SWORN TO before me, Notary Public for and in the
City/Municipality of _Ormoc City, Leyte_ this _ _day of_

PAGE NO. _____
BOOK NO. _____
Series of _____

fig 2.2

"This is a splinter of impressions you know you will never forget. You repeat the memory when you sleep. The memory repeats." ~Mg Roberts

A moment of absolute horror. Peripheral vision disappears. Flames sharpen. I do not want ashes. *I want to dance the hostility of the universe.* Blow out the flames with three deep dragon breaths. *I want to dance the shame from my body.* They keep burning. The edges curl. *I want a doorway.* Throw the paper on the wet ground. Stomp on it. *I want to dance out of this earth and into another.* Muddy footprints splatter. Arms above head like jungle crow wings. *I want to be the one who controls where I am going.* Place the paper on top of a blank notebook. *I want to dance myself into a new story.* Burnt flakes carry off in the wind. *A place where I only know of ordinary things.*

I want to dance the hostility of the universe.

Riomaggioremeans"majorriver"oneoftheItaliancoastaltownsofCinqueterre"five earths"becausethisiswherethefiveearthsmergethisiswherepastelhousesreachup-the hillstowardstheUniversebelowthereisbarkingdoriesswishintheharborfish-ermen castnetscatchdrunkAmericangirlstakethemtothebeachaholeintherocks-theygethigh theysing *donttellmeifImdying…ifIcan'tseethesun,maybeIshouldgo…"*

Rough hands and salt breath. Fingers grip. Neck. Arms. Push against. Hunger. Touch. Up shirt. Down pants. Unable. To move. To speak. Awareness. Of body. Of breasts. Of a current. Between thighs.

I dissipate.

A body becomes just a body. A body that is just a body can be passed around.

A barefoot girl in a black dress twirls in the moonshine. She has long black hair.
It sways in the breeze.

It whispers: *Peace*   *Peace*   *Peace*

The smell of the Tyrrhenian Sea lingers.

In a poem called "The Same Old Figurative," Joel M. Toledo writes:

> Come the divining
> can wait.
> Let us examine the wreckage.

I want to dance the shame from my body.

Reflections glare off surfaces. Distorted. Bent. When I left the Philippines, my birth country, I did not leave behind the dark crimson line. It followed me through the gray walls of the orphanage to the laminate white-tan floors of my last foster home through six transnational moves and back again. Unintentionally I traced then reenacted my mother's trauma. The result of Riomaggiore is my secret. In the same way I am my mother's secret.

Two years ago, during a return trip in the Philippines, I took a 14-hour ferry ride from Cebu to Iloilo. Staring out into the sea I noticed there was no horizon, no vanishing point, to distinguish black water from black sky. Black is an absence of light that makes invisible the bruise from the connective tissue through to the very white marrow of the spine. And when the blackness becomes unspoken and cannot be dispersed from the body the next of kin inherits it. And it continues. This is how my mother's shame becomes mine. But my shame will not become his. I am my mother, but I'm not.

DECLARATION OF IDENTITY FOR VISA PURPOSES

I hereby declare that the following particulars concerning myself are true:-

NAME IN FULL	MARILYN MALINAO		
OCCUPATION	CHILD	RESIDENCE	USA
PLACE AND DATE OF BIRTH	ORMOC CITY, PHILIPPINES	30 AUGUST 1985	

(Name)	(Date of birth)
CHILDREN ACCOMPANYING (IF ANY)	

DESCRIPTION	Height	4	
	Colour of eyes	BROWN	
	Colour of hair	BLACK	
	Special Peculiarities	—	

SIGNATURE OF TRAVELLER

WITNESS OF SIGNATURE

(Stamp)

COPY

VISAS

DOFI A/L 440526

ENTRY CERTIFICATE
VISA VISIT
SINGLE ENTRY
Valid for presentation at a United
Kingdom port until
10 DEC 1993 (Date)
provided this passport remains valid.
SIGNED
DATE JUN 1 0 1993

BRITISH CONSULATE-GENERAL
NEW YORK

LEAVE TO ENTER FOR SIX MONTHS
EMPLOYMENT PROHIBITED

IMMIGRATION OFFICER
11 JUN 1993
HEATHROW (3)

fig 2.3

I want a doorway.

A dream whisper says, *you must dig down to find the land whose soil from which you are made.*

A bamboo tree spends four years traveling down into the depths of blackness to establish roots. Then, in its fifth year, it breaks through the surface and in less than six weeks grows 90-feet towards the mystical heavens.

To dig is to touch. Touch is a form of deepening. Touch is what anchors you to your body.

What if I am afraid to be anchored?

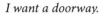

I want to dance out of this earth and into another.

It would be a simple place. In the Philippines. A small town called Alinao in the province of Albay, situated along the coast of Lagonoy Gulf to the east and Mount Malinao, a dormant volcano, to the west. At the base of this volcano, in a small bahay kubo, would live a brown-skinned little girl named Luzvaminda and everyone would call her Luz.

Luz loves to climb balete trees and irritate the duwende that live there. She loves to steam suman malagkit, sweet rice wrapped in banana leaves, in the earth. And she loves the smell of white sampaguitas and the jungle after it rains. Though unable to read, she holds three songs in her heart: one for her family, one for seafaring strangers, and one for the tangerine moon at night.

At the Babaylan Conference, I learned Malinao also means 'an abundance of Alinao'. A native plant, alinao is a small shrub or tree with small pale blue flowers and purplish-red berries.

Immediately, I begin to research it, but it disappeared sometime between the Spanish-American War of 1898, in which the United States won thus gaining the Philippines as a territory, and the subsequent Philippine-American War, which lasted from 1899 to 1902.

The last time it is mentioned is in a book compiled by Elmer D. Merrill, a botanist who worked for the newly established government.

I don't want to disappear.

LUZ

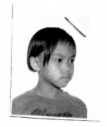

EMBASSY OF THE PHILIPPINES
9A Palace Green, London W8 4QE

REGISTRATION OF FILIPINO NATIONALS

Name: MARILYN MARINAO   Age: 7

Civil Status: Single (X) Married ( ) Separated ( ) Divorced ( )

Married to   :

Place of Birth: ORMOC CITY   Date of Birth: 08-30-85

Passport No. :   Issued in MANILLA

      on   .

Immigration Status: Permanent Resident ( ) Contract Worker ( ) Visitor (X)

            Student ( ) Seamen ( ) Others ( )

Occupation/Profession :

Date of Arrival in U.K.: 06.11.93.

Address in U.K.: Home :

COPY

fig 2.4

I want to be the one who controls where I am going.

When I was a child in England, deported there from the US due to misplaced paperwork, I lived at the Grange in Long Wittenham with my Aunty and Uncle. On my way to the local primary school, I often took a detour so I could walk along the Thames. I liked to collect four leaf clovers and tape them in my notebook made out of loose leaf paper stapled together.

With words, I only documented Saturdays. Before afternoon tea. When we would visit the thoroughbreds. My favorite was Chestnut who was golden brown with a blond mane. Sometimes I would decorate his hooves with glittery nail polish. Sometimes I would kiss his nose. Sometimes, as we trotted around the track, I would stretch out my arms like jungle crow wings and let myself sink into him, my body swaying to match the rhythm of his.

mother: adelia

mother: rosita

mother: marites

mother: elsa

mother: marilyn

mother: natasha

mother: jane

mother: jocelyn

mother: grace

mother: arline

mother: mary

mother

mother   mother
mother   mother
mother   mother   mother
          mother   mother   mother
mother mother mother   mother   mother mother mother   mother mother
m o t h e r m o t h e r m o t h e r   m o t h e r   m o t h e r mother m
themthermothermothermothermothermothermothermothermothermot her moth
ermothermothermothermothermothermothermothermothermothermother
mothermothermothermothermother   mother mo ther mothermotherm
othermothermothermothermothermothermothermothermot m o t h e r m
o t h e r m o t h e r m o t h e r m o t h e r m o t h e r m o t h e
r mothermothermothermothermothermothermothermothermothermothermother
mothermothermothermothermothermothermothermothermothermothermother
motherm   othermotherm   othermothermothermothermothermo
therm other mothermothermothermothermothermothermothermothermother
mothermother mothermothermothermotherm
          otherm othermothermothermothermothermother
mothermothermo thermothermothermothermothermothermothermothermother
mothermothermothermothermothermothermother   mother
mother mothermothermothermothermothermothermothermothermothermother
mothermot
m o t h e r m o t h e r m o t h e r m o t h e r m o t h e r m o t h e r m o t h e r
mothermotherm othermothermothermothermothermothermothermother
mothermothermothermothermothermotherm othermothermothermothermother
mothermotherm othermothermothermothermothermothermothermothermother
mothermothermothermothermotherm   othermother
  mother   mother mothermotherm

          othermothermotherm othermothermothermothermothermothermothermot m o t
h e r m o t h e r m o t h e r m o   t   h   e   r   m   o
t   h   e   r   m   o   t   h   e   r
  m   o   t   h   e   r mothermothermothermothermo
thermothermothermothermothermother mothermothermothermotherm
othermothermotherm othermothermotherm other

In December of last year we returned to England. Because Gran had terminal cancer. All the horses were gone and the track lines were barely visible beneath the tall grasses and weeds that reclaimed it.

mothermothermothermothermothermothermothermothermothermothermother

I want to dance myself into a new story.

On a scrap of paper I wrote three names of people whose deaths I witnessed, but whose bodies I never buried. And I watched it burn. To ashes. In a Charnel Ground, a rectangular structure made of bricks painted white. Afterwards, I lay in it, staring up at the orange clouds and azure sky through a rusted red grate.

Do not name the dead. Are you ready? Are you willing to let them go?

At the mall, someone mistakes my friend for my adoptive mother's daughter: "your daughter looks beautiful in that dress."

My mother says, "she isn't my daughter," and walks over to me, arm around my shoulders, "this... this is my daughter."

'Amanda' means 'worthy of love.'

My birth mother's name was Adelia Malinao. My name was Marilyn Malinao. His name was

fig 2.5

A place where I only know of ordinary things.

I catch the bus to school and walk through the white door of the greenhouse, saying softly, *tabi-tabi po*, to excuse myself for disturbing the duwende. Through the fiberglass dome the light slants sideways.

Plants are physical and ethereally sensitive beings. Yesterday, I planted basil in a pastel yellow pot and put it on my window sill. Like the locals do in Greece. For good luck and to ward off evil. But I was feeling ashamed and curled up in a fetal position, the blanket up over my head. This morning I found the basil had shriveled too.

The name I go by now is 'Ngoho.' It is a verb. It is the act of bringing the spirit down into the physical body. Through sitting. In a grounded way. Have you ever lay down in the grass and gazed at the sky? 'Ngoho' is that sudden feeling, after laying for a long time, of the earth opening up to cradle you. The way a mother would.

In the greenhouse, I kneel down next to the lemon tree. To cleanse the body. I force myself to relax clenched fists. To touch the damp soil. To touch the shiny, dark green leaves. To touch brings about new bodies and territories. The branches hang low from the weight of its fruit.

APPENDIX: *NOTES TOWARDS TESSERAE*

In January 2013, having just returned from celebrating the holidays with some of my dad's family in England, I walked into the first day of Bhanu Kapil's Experimental Prose class full of suspicion and reverse culture shock. As way to approach our first text, she asked us to walk towards red and gather notes. Though initially a failure, I came away from this with a fragment: "my wanting is not the grid's wanting." How the city is set up to control one's movements through it. How institutions are made not for the immigrants and orphans that move through them, but for the sake of efficiency. Unbeknownst to me, it became the groundwork for a journey through dreamtime and a question asked months later after stumbling upon Bernard Tschumi's "The Architectural Paradox." I wondered: what is the difference between the architecture [institution] itself and the body that moves through it?

Within the following two weeks of that walk, I had my first of many defining moments and met a Shaman in a coffee shop. Having recently begun reading Kapil's Schizophrene, the book was sitting on the table. The Shaman noticed it and shared her own personal experience with schizophrenia and immigration. In turn, I shared my immigration/ adoption story from the Philippines and showed her how, in the middle of my palm, the leaves of a balete tree can transform into birds. She brought my birth mother's spirit into the room, hugged me and said, "names change and it's okay. I'm living my third name and you're walking towards your first." During the entire three or so hours we chatted, no one entered the coffee shop and I had moments where I thought perhaps I am hallucinating the whole thing. Before she left, she said that if I ever needed her again to go up into the mountains, shout her name and ask my question(s). But every time I go I doubt her existence and the questions get caught in my throat. If I had the courage, I would shout towards the heavens: where am I from and whom do I look like?

Origin Story

Five hours by ferry from mainland Athens, at a bar called Meltemi, I tried to comfort a friend who then turned to me all glasseyed and said, "you'll never understand the pressures parents put on their children. You don't have parents. Your family isn't your real

---

1 The Tagalog phrase, *Pagtatanim ng Binhi*, means "planting the seeds," and was the title of the first full day of the 2nd International Babaylan Conference held in Westminster Woods near Occidental, Sonoma County, California from 27 Sept. through 29 Sept. 2013. The second full day was titled Anihan, which means "harvest," or "gathering the seeds." The conference itself was called *Katutubong Binhi/ Native Seeds: Myths and Stories that Feed our Indigenous Soul.*

family." Although such comments are not foreign to me, I have never had someone close to me say something like this. Speechless, I slammed my beer on the table and walked out across the ring road to the coastline. Watching the evening ferry to Athens disappear into a sea of blackness, I felt the return of the age old question of nurture versus nature. I remembered Ireland.

It was not until high school that I truly felt different from my family. Nine of us, from my (adopted) mother's side, went to Ireland to research family roots. We traced the entire perimeter, starting in Dublin, then going north near Ballintoy in N. Ireland, west to Galway, south to Blarney and up again to Dublin. We visited the remnants of an old castle that supposedly belonged to one of our ancestors. My cousin, eleven at the time, cried and said, "this is where we come from. Can you feel it? The land." And I also cried, told her yes, but secretly felt shocked I did not feel the same connection, that my body did not respond to the land the same way. Then, a few years later, while living in Greece, a Filipina poet and neighbor said, "you've never returned to the Philippines?" and invited me to go stay with her and her family. And a year after that, I returned for the first time and upon stepping off the plane at once understood what it was my cousin had felt in Ireland. How the humidity hit my face. How the ground hummed.

In Journey of the Adopted Self: A Quest for Wholeness[2], Betty Jean Lifton recalls a story told to her by an adopted woman named Lee. Lee says, "the story about who we are is a sacred story. When people take it or keep it from us, they rob us of ourselves. They destroy the most sacred thing of all. They kill our Source." She continues on to share the cultural tradition of adoption in Native American society, which she had learned from recently working on a reservation:

"if you rear someone else's child and that child is of the Bear Clan and you're of the Turtle Clan, you've got to tell him what it means to be of the Bear Clan. He's got to be given a name that fits with Bear Clan customs. He's got to know that he's got his whole identity and that identity goes right back to the myth, right back to the beginning of time."[3]

These stories not only tell us who we are but also connects us to something bigger: our indigenous memory and spiritual heritage. It places us in the great cosmic wheel.[4]

2 Betty Jean Lifton, Journey of the Adopted Self: A Quest for Wholeness (New York, NY: Basic, 1994), 37.
3 Ibid, 3738.
4 In The Man Made of Words: Essays, Stories, Passages, N. Scott Momaday describes a pilgrimage tracing his native Kiowa roots across North America. In the Bighorn Mountains, near the MontanaWyoming border, is a Medicine Wheel fifty feet in diameter. He writes: "We do not know as a matter of fact who made this wheel or to what purpose. [...] What we know without doubt is that it is a sacred expression, an equation of man's relation to the cosmos" (120).

Throughout this project, I have been thinking about trauma and institutions. During research into attachment theory and its relationship to time spent in the child welfare system, I stumbled upon a book titled *Healing Developmental Trauma: How Early Trauma Affects Self Regulation, SelfImage, and the Capacity for Relationship* by Laurence Heller, PhD, and Aline LaPierre, PsyD. They introduce the NeuroAffective Relational Model (NARM), a simultaneous topdown, bottomup, somatic psychotherapeutic model that builds upon Peter Levine's work on somatic experiencing.[5]

Studies in developmental trauma show a relationship between early neglect and its negative effects on brain development, the nervous system, and the endocrine system. There is a direct correlational relationship between time spent in an orphanage and/or foster care, and the child's reactivity and sensitivity to emotional information, sensory stimulation, and anxiety levels[6] [sometimes (mis)diagnosed as attachment disorder or institutional autism].[7] And because this early trauma occurs before the brain is fully developed, the memories are stored implicitly as immobilized energy.[8] The consequences include dissociation, including numbing, splitting and fragmentation; freezing; contraction and withdrawal; and the inability to connect to the self and others.

To move towards connection, NARM introduces NeuroAffective Touch, a physical and direct contact approach combined with somatic conversations between the client and the therapist. In a TINGE Magazine interview, Bhanu Kapil says, "In Schizophrene I wanted, too, to think about how[...] a touch that repeats, [...] a light touch — is healing, too. It can bring you back."[9] But what if, due to experience, one learns not to trust touch? What if, even if she desires touch, she recoils from it?

On 13 October 2013, Kapil led a workshop in Loveland, Colorado on bibliomancy, a divinatory art where one meditates on a question, closes her eyes, orients to a book and then points to a passage in it. During the meditation, I asked "how do I continue?" and saw a leaf with a black center and shimmery edges. When I oriented to the book, I thought I was orienting to the section on science, but ended up in a section on spirituality and grief.

---

5 I first learned of Levine and his work in Bhanu Kapil's Experimental Prose class in Spring 2013. To learn about somatic experiencing, refer to Levine's book, Waking the Tiger: Healing Trauma : The Innate Capacity to Transform Overwhelming Experiences (Berkeley, CA: North Atlantic, 1997).

6 Nim Tottenham, "Human Amygdala Development in the Absence of SpeciesExpected Caregiving" (Los Angeles: Wiley Periodicals, Inc., 2011).

7 Boris Gindis, Ph.D., LP, "Institutional Autism in Children Adopted Internationally: Myth or Reality?" (International Journal of Special Education, Vol. 23, No. 3, 2008), 118123.

8 Levine, 2022.

9 "An Interview with Bhanu Kapil." Interview by Stephanie Luczajko. TINGE Magazine, Issue 2, Fall 2011. Web. 18 Nov. 2013. <http://www.tingemagazine.org/aninterviewwithbhanukapi/>.

The hardcover book, **When Women Were Birds** by Terry Tempest Williams, was propped up on a bookstand and I felt it staring right into me. I pointed to the passage that read:

"A mother and daughter are an edge. Edges are ecotones, transitional zones, places of danger or opportunity. Housedwelling tension. When I stand on the edge of the land and sea, I feel this tension, this fluid line of transition."[10]

Though unsure what this meant, I knew it was important. Within the past year, one of my childhood spirit animals, the crow, had returned in a significant way to my life and in addition, I had been unsuccessfully writing about the birthmother/daughter relationship since the beginning of my journey at Naropa University. Cixous asks, "Why is it so difficult to write?"[11] Supposing that the act of writing is an architectural site, Bernard Tschumi answers: "Architecture is the ultimate erotic act. Carry it to excess and it will reveal both the traces of reason and the sensual experience of space. Simultaneously." [12] In other words, as Elizabeth Grosz writes, "the fabrication of space [is where] sensations may emerge."[13] The frame reveals sensations and, because trauma is "held in the nervous system, not the event,"[14] these sensations give rise to traumatic memory stored implicitly. As such, I fear certain memories might become explicit and therefore recoiled, subconsciously sabotaging my own writing.

In "Mourning and Its Relation to ManicDepressive States," Melanie Klein states, "When the depressive position arises, the ego is forced [...] to develop methods of defence which are essentially directed against the 'pining' for the love object."[15] How desire and anger are siblings. Anger as a defence mechanism against grief. How I want my birth mother, but refuse and resist becoming her. And how, in the refusal, I unintentionally mirrored her. The blackness[16] of the sea is also the trace of ancestral trauma inherited through mitochondrial DNA, the umbilical cord. How we are left to process it through subconscious reenactment and thereby ancestral trauma becomes personal. The need to discharge the growing, yet immobilized energy becomes even more urgent and necessary. Desire overcomes fear.

But how is this done? How do I continue?

10 Terry Tempest Williams, When Women Were Birds: Fiftyfour Variations on Voice (New York: Sarah Crichton, 2012), 20.
11 Cixous, 107.
12 Bernard Tschumi, Advertisements for Architecture (1975).
13 Elizabeth Grosz, Chaos, Territory, Art: Deleuze and the Framing of the Earth (New York: Columbia University Press, 2008), 12.
14 From a lecture by guest Laura Campbell, M.A. Transpersonal Counseling Psychology, an advanced practitioner of somatic experiencing. She visited Bhanu Kapil's "Experimental Prose" class on 11 March 2013.
15 Melanie Klein, "Mourning and Its Relation to ManicDepressive States," Essential Papers on Object Loss, by Rita V. Frankiel (New York: New York UP, 1994), 95122.
16 From Hélène Cixous' Stigmata: Escaping Texts: "I say blackness, and not: black. Blackness isn't black. It is the last degree of reds. The secret blood of reds" (4).

I do not remember years, but I do remember three labyrinths. The first was in Milwaukee, Wisconsin. I was 22 or 23 years old and participating in a women's only creative healing support group. The green duct tape was strategically placed on the floor of a gym. Music played in the background.

One of the group facilitators explained that a labyrinth was different from a maze. A labyrinth is meant to guide; a maze is meant to confuse. This was a test in trusting the labyrinth. We were to write what we wanted to let go of on a slip of paper and meditate on it as we walked to the middle where we burned it. Then walk out. As an act of catharsis, I wrote "anger" and burned it easily, but on my way out I panicked. The singer on the audio cd was singing something about coming home and, as someone who has moved and traveled several times across countries and continents, I felt split. What or to which home did this singer refer? Catharsis, but then what? And so the labyrinth became the thing to figure out and a trope, a word that comes from the Greek τρόπος (tropos), meaning "way" or "direction," towards home, wherever that may be. I began wearing a labyrinth pendant on a black cord around my neck until, at 25, I came upon my second labyrinth.

I was living in Paroikia, a port town on Paros, a cycladic island in the middle of the Aegean Sea, in attempt to avoid a graduate degree in creative writing at Naropa University. I had recently learned how one might weave the wind into a blanket to keep warm and thus felt safe when caught between the meltemi, a dry northerly wind often blamed for the increase of depression and suicide; and the scirocco, a harsh and humid wind carrying red dust from Morocco to Italy, often blamed for crimes of passion. I planned to take the ferry to Crete, famous for its stories of the labyrinth and the Minotaur, after a fisherman tenderizing octopi by slamming it against Parian marble told me the story of Ariadne and Theseus: Ariadne's father, King Minos of Crete, had Daedalus build a labyrinth to hide the Minotaur, a half man half bull offspring of Minos' wife Pasiphae and a bull. Every nine years, King Minos sent seven men and women to the Minotaur as sacrifice. One year, an Athenian named Theseus volunteered to slay the Minotaur and Ariadne, in love with him, gave him a spool of thread to unwind through the labyrinth so he could find his way back out.

---

17 Three times I have encountered the thread during my journey at Naropa University: first, in the classroom as part of Bhanu Kapil's practice with red thread; second, in Cecilia Vicuña's workshop during Week Four of Naropa's 2013 Summer Writing Program; and third, just after Christmas 2013, while contemplating the labyrinth (via Cixous and Tschumi), I encountered BBC's new show, Atlantis. The pilot episode was a remixing of the tale of Ariadne and Theseus, a story I've only heard once before from a fisherman in Greece. I began to think about the labyrinths, in the traditional sense of the word, that have made a lasting impression in my life.

Because of previous experience with the labyrinth, this story moved me and I desperately wanted to see the myth's origin site. However, standing outside of the Cave of the Nymphs on the day I was to leave, I brought my hand up to touch my labyrinth pendant and found it had fallen off. I took this as a sign and did not go.

Then, three years later, after turning 28, I came upon my third labyrinth during the 2nd International Babaylan Conference. Geared towards Filipinos in the diaspora and allies, this conference focused on katutubong binhi (native seeds), in particular, indigenous storytelling and mythmaking (i.e. dream space). Skipping one of the presentations, I put on my Kalinga clothes and hiked along the creek with a new *diwata* inspired friend until we reached the labyrinth. Feeling illequipped, I did not enter. Instead I watched my friend walk the whorls and looped lines as if the labyrinth were a thumbmark of a forgotten cultural heritage.

In hindsight, I wonder now about the significance of dream space. If it is true that, as Bernard Tschumi writes, "the labyrinth is such that it entertains dreams,"[18] and that, as Hélène Cixous writes, the "text is a labyrinth,"[19] then what are these dream spaces and what role do they play in our immigrant narratives? As a child, I quite often live(d) in dreamed up spaces and, having participated in the Babaylan Conference, I know there are others who live(d) similarly. Why do we create these dream spaces? Why are they so prevalent in our narratives? I think it is not only a way to make trauma bearable, but also allows us to journey to the center of the labyrinth and face the Minotaur (the blackness in the center of the leaf with shimmery edges). This journey, a spiral dance, is a remembering of the body, or a weaving between fragmented memories and stories with which we must reconcile. It is only after that we can return. Can we return? Tschumi writes, "The dark corners of experience are not unlike a labyrinth, where all sensations, all feelings are enhanced, but where no overview is present to provide a clue about how to get out."[20] How do we get out? Per the story of Ariadne, Cixous writes,

"one must enter the labyrinth of a text with a thread."[21]

What does this thread look like? I believe the truest thread is unique to each person. In Bhanu Kapil's Schizophrene, it is "light touch." For me, it is through the stories embedded in my birth surname, Malinao. During my journey, starting with the return trip to the Philippines in 2011 through to the end of my time at Naropa, I have learned that Alinao is a town that lies between Lagonoy Gulf to the east and Mount Malinao, a volcano, to the

18 Bernard Tschumi, "The Architectural Paradox," Studio International (SeptemberOctober 1975). 19 Cixous, 139.
20 Tschumi. See: above.
21 Cixous, 139.

west in the province of Albay. Malinao has two stories: first, it is a portmanteau of ma alinao, which means "an abundance of alinao." A native plant, alinao is a small shrub or tree with small pale blue flowers and purplish-red berries. I tried to find out more but it disappears from books around the turn of the last century. It is last mentioned in A Dictionary of the Plant Names of the Philippine Islands compiled by botanist Elmer D. Merrill,[22] and printed by the newly established government in 1903. Incidentally, this is also around the time of the SpanishAmerican War of 1898, in which the United States won thus gaining the Philippines as a territory, and the subsequent PhilippineAmerican War, which lasted from 1899 to 1902.

The second meaning of Malinao is "clear." The story follows that Arimaonga, the lion of the sky, attempts to swallow the moon during a lunar eclipse. While my ancestors dance and play drums to scare him away, the Moros cross the sea with their barongs stained red and kill all but seven women. The Moros rape, then take the women on their out-rigger canoe. Wishing to die rather than become slaves, the women sing canticles. And in these canticles are such 'clear thoughts' (in local bikolnaga: malinao na isip) the boat sinks, their captors drown and from the seafloor rises an island. The surviving women climb upon this island and become clairvoyants.

It is through this origin story, my birth culture's stories and myths, and plant spir-it dreaming that I can find my 'way' (tropos) and reconnect. Anihan, a Tagalog word meaning "gathering the seeds," refers to the harvest during which farmers gather the fruits of their labour. I imagine each seed is a tessera (pl. tesserae), an island, one of the small tiles of stone or glass that makes up a mosaic, an archipelago. And I imagine each tessera represented by a sentence or a fragment or a memory or a story that makes up my narrative. In this project, I attempt to gather seeds. To heal. To dance in and towards wholeness.[23] This is both my dream space and my thread. I make my way as I go.

Amanda [Ngoho] Reavey

22 Elmer D Merrill, Dep. of the Interior: Bureau of Gov. Laboratories; A Dictionary of the Native Plant Names of the Philippine Islands (Manila: Bureau of Publ. Print., 1903), 5.
23 Agnes MiclatCacayan, "She Dances in Wholeness," Babaylan: Filipinos and the Call of the Indigenous. By Leny Mendoza Strobel. (Davao City, Philippines: Ateneo De Davao University, Research and Publica-tions Office, 2010), 119.

ACKNOWLEDGMENTS

Infinite thanks and love to my parents, Pat and Mary Reavey.

Thank you to the Naropa faculty and staff, especially my professor and thesis advisor Bhanu Kapil. Without her push, support and critique, I would never have written this, nor have had the courage. Also, during my time at Naropa, I read Bhanu's Schizophrene, which introduced me to "light touch." Any time I felt I couldn't continue, I re-read it.

Thank you to all of my fellow Naropians especially my classmates in the Spring 2013 Experimental Prose and Fall 2013 Memoir/Anti-memoir classes. A very special thanks to Celia Seaton, April Joseph, June Lucarotti, Peggy Alaniz, Ashley Waterman, Sarah Richards Graba, and Eric Fischman. Thank you Kyle Pivarnik for your support, and to Andrea Rexilius for the purple couch. I also want to thank Maureen Owen who went out of her way to track me down when I "disappeared" from the MFA online program.

Thank you Erica Hocking and Sherry Gobaleza for the garden and greenhouse magics! Thank you Naropa Greenhouse and everyone involved with the Center for Babaylan Studies. Especially, maraming salamat po   Ate Leny Strobel and Ate Mila Anguluan Coger!

Thank you Jen Hofer, Lisa Birman, Mg Roberts, Larissa Lai, Carmen Giménez Smith, Melissa R. Sipin and Eileen Tabios for your support and for reading my manuscript in different stages. Thanks to Franklin R. Cline, Charles Alexander, Curtis Romero, Mairead Case for scrutinizing over a single page. Thank you Amy Catanzano for your support, for reading my manuscript and writing a blurb!

Eileen Tabios, thank you for publishing an excerpt in Galatea Resurrects #23. Thanks to Construction Literary Magazine for publishing "Emigrant Notes on Possession" in their Winter 2015 issue, and to Joshua Marie Wilkinson and Afton Wilky for publishing a poetics essay that contained excerpts from Marilyn in Issue #50.

Thank you also to Meaghan Owens, my best friend and kindred spirit, to whom this book is dedicated, for the phrases "chicory moon," and "plants are physical and ethereally sensitive beings."Also, on page 54, the centered italics are an excerpt from When Women Were Birds by Terry Tempest Williams.

Thank you to Joel M. Toledo for giving us permission to use The Same Old Figurative (p.51), a poem I carried for so long.

Thank you to Nikay Paredes and her family, and my second foster family, the Jeremiejczyks, for hosting me in the Philippines and in Australia.

Thank you to JooYoung Choi for her amazing work and for letting me use her painting for the book cover. And lastly thank you Lynne DeSilva-Johnson and The Operating System Press for publishing Marilyn and giving me this chance.

Bahala na.

Born in the Philippines, raised in Wisconsin, Amanda [Ngoho] Reavey is a poet, a Reiki practitioner and a cellist interested in plant spirit communication and healing.

A graduate of the MFA Writing & Poetics program at Naropa University, her work appears in Construction Magazine, Galatea Resurrects #23 and The Volta, among others.

Reavey currently works as Marketing Director at Woodland Pattern Book Center. MARILYN is her first book.

Find her at spaceinsideborderline.com.

Through painting, video, sculpture, animation, and music, multi-disciplinary artist JooYoung Choi documents the interconnecting narratives of a highly-structured, expansive fictional land called the Cosmic Womb. This paracosm stretches over approximately 6,732 miles, and is governed by Queen Kiok, with the help of six humanoid creatures called Tuplets (Lady K, Aidee Three, Emo Flowers (No. 36), Kun-Yook Six, Lydia "Nine" Fletcher, Haneul-Sek aka Nina Blue and one Earthling from Concord, NH named C.S. Watson.) Guided by the Cosmic Womb mythology, Choi creates work that merges the autobiographic with the fantastic into a visual form.

The narrative of this imaginary world is used as a tool to investigate a variety of themes such as: representation as affirmation, racism and systemic oppression, personal/political identity and memory.

Her work intends specifically to:
1. Address challenging issues through playful narratives,
2. Develop formally compelling imagery, *and to*
3. Engage viewers in a manner that is accessible and invokes curiosity, learning, and discourse.

JooYoung Choi, born in Seoul, South Korea, immigrated to Concord, New Hampshire in 1983 by way of adoption. While completing her BFA at Massachusetts College of Art and Design, she returned to South Korea and reunited with her birth-family. Since receiving her MFA from Lesley University in Cambridge, Massachusetts, Choi's artwork has been exhibited in such venues as The Wing Luke Museum of the Asian Pacific American Experience, Seattle, Washington; The National Museum of Mexican Art, Chicago, Illinois; and Lawndale Art Center, Houston, Texas. Choi's work has been featured by numerous media groups and publications, including the Korean Global News Network YTN, Houston's PaperCity, Nat. Brut, and Huffington Post. She is an Artadia finalist for 2015.

www.jooyoungchoi.com

THIS is not a fixed entity.

The OS is an ongoing experiment in resilient creative practice which necessarily morphs as its conditions and collaborators change. It is not a magazine, a website, or a press, but rather an ongoing dialogue ABOUT the act of publishing on and offline: it is an exercise in the use and design of both of these things and their role in our shifting cultural landscape, explored THROUGH these things.

I see publication as documentation: an act of resistance, an essential community process, and a challenge to the official story / archive, and I founded the OS to exemplify my belief that people everywhere can train themselves to use self or community documentation as the lifeblood of a resilient, independent, successful creative practice.

The name "THE OPERATING SYSTEM" is meant to speak to an understanding of the self as a constantly evolving organism, which just like any other system needs to learn to adapt if it is to survive. Just like your computer, you need to be "updating your software" frequently, as your patterns and habits no longer serve you.

Our intentions above all are empowerment and unsilencing, encouraging creators of all ages and colors and genders and backgrounds and disciplines to reclaim the rights to cultural storytelling, and in so doing to the historical record of our times and lives.

Bob Holman once told me I was "scene agnostic" and I took this as the highest compliment: indeed, I seek work and seek to make and promote work that will endure and transcend tastes and trends, making important and asserting value rather than being told was has and has not.

The OS has evolved in quite a short time from an idea to a growing force for change and possibility: in a span of 5 years, from 2013-2017, we will have published more than 40 volumes from a hugely diverse group of contributors, and solicited and curated thousands of pieces online, collaborating with artists, composers, choreographers, scientists, futurists, and so many more. On-line, you'll also find partnerships with cultural organizations modelling the value of archival process documentation.

Beginning in 2016, our new series :: "Glossarium: Unsilenced Texts and Modern Translations", will bring on Ariel Resnikoff, Stephen Ross, and Mona Kareem as contributing editors, and have as its first volume a dual language translation of Palestinian poet and artist Ashraf Fayadh's "Instructions Within," translated by Mona Kareem, which will be published later this year, with all proceeds going to support Fayadh's ongoing case and imprisonment in Saudi Arabia.

There is ample room here for you to expand and grow your practice ...and your possibility. Join us.

- Lynne DeSilva-Johnson,
Founder and Managing Editor

DOC U MENT
/däky ə m ənt/

First meant "instruction" or "evidence," whether written or not.

noun - a piece of written, printed, or electronic matter that provides information or evidence or that serves as an official record
verb - record (something) in written, photographic, or other form
synonyms - paper - deed - record - writing - act - instrument

[*Middle English, precept, from Old French, from Latin documentum, example, proof, from docre, to teach; see dek- in Indo-European roots.*]

Who is responsible for the manufacture of value?

Based on what supercilious ontology have we landed in a space where we vie against other creative people in vain pursuit of the fleeting credibilities of the scarcity economy, rather than freely collaborating and sharing openly with each other in ecstatic celebration of MAKING?

While we understand and acknowledge the economic pressures and fear-mongering that threatens to dominate and crush the creative impulse, we also believe that now more than ever we have the tools to relinquish agency via cooperative means,
fueled by the fires of the Open Source Movement.

**Looking out across the invisible vistas of that rhizomatic parallel country
we can begin to see our community beyond constraints,
in the place where intention meets resilient, proactive, collaborative organization.**

Here is a document born of that belief, sown purely of imagination and will.
When we document we assert. We print to make real, to reify our being there.
When we do so with mindful intention to address our process,
to open our work to others, to create beauty in words in space, to respect and acknowledge the
strength of the page we now hold physical, a thing in our hand...
we remind ourselves that, like Dorothy: *we had the power all along, my dears.*

the PRINT! DOCUMENT SERIES

is a project of
Lynne DeSilva-Johnson, Curator and Editor

produced and published for

the operating system